Goblin Market

CHRISTINA ROSSETTI

A Phoenix Paperback

Poems and Prose by Christina Rossetti first published
by J. M. Dent in 1994

This abridged edition published in 1996 by Phoenix
a division of Orion Books Ltd
Orion House, 5 Upper St Martin's Lane, London WC2H 9EA

Copyright © Orion Books Ltd 1996

Cover illustration: *Reverie* by Dante Gabriel Rossetti © Christie's
Colour Library, London (Bridgeman Art Library, London)

ISBN 1 85799 557 0

Typeset by Deltatype Ltd, Ellesmere Port, Cheshire
Printed in Great Britain by Clays Ltd, St Ives plc.

Contents

Song

When I am dead, my dearest,
   Sing no sad songs for me;
Plant thou no roses at my head,
   Nor shady cypress tree:
Be the green grass above me
   With showers and dewdrops wet;
And if thou wilt, remember,
   And if thou wilt, forget.

I shall not see the shadows,
   I shall not feel the rain;
I shall not hear the nightingale
   Sing on, as if in pain:
And dreaming through the twilight
   That doth not rise nor set,
Haply I may remember,
   And haply may forget.

Remember

Remember me when I am gone away,
　　Gone far away into the silent land;
　　When you can no more hold me by the hand,
Nor I half turn to go yet turning stay.
Remember me when no more day by day
　　You tell me of our future that you planned:
　　Only remember me; you understand
It will be late to counsel then or pray.
Yet if you should forget me for a while
　　And afterwards remember, do not grieve:
　　For if the darkness and corruption leave
　　A vestige of the thoughts that once I had,
Better by far you should forget and smile
　　Than you should remember and be sad.

Echo

Come to me in the silence of the night;
    Come in the speaking silence of a dream;
Come with soft rounded cheeks and eyes as bright
    As sunlight on a stream;
        Come back in tears,
O memory, hope, love of finished years.

Oh dream how sweet, too sweet, too bitter sweet,
    Whose wakening should have been in Paradise,
Where souls brimfull of love abide and meet;
    Where thirsting longing eyes
        Watch the slow door
That opening, letting in, lets out no more.

Yet come to me in dreams, that I may live
    My very life again tho' cold in death:
Come back to me in dreams, that I may give
    Pulse for pulse, breath for breath:
        Speak low, lean low,
As long ago, my love, how long ago.

Memory

I

I nursed it in my bosom while it lived,
  I hid it in my heart when it was dead;
In joy I sat alone, even so I grieved
    Alone and nothing said.

I shut the door to face the naked truth,
  I stood alone – I faced the truth alone,
Stripped bare of self-regard or forms or ruth
    Till first and last were shown.

I took the perfect balances and weighed;
  No shaking of my hand disturbed the poise;
Weighed, found it wanting: not a word I said,
    But silent made my choice.

None know the choice I made; I make it still.
  None know the choice I made and broke my heart,
Breaking mine idol: I have braced my will
    Once, chosen for once my part.

I broke it at a blow, I laid it cold,
  Crushed in my deep heart where it used to live.
My heart dies inch by inch; the time grows old,
    Grows old in which I grieve.

A Birthday

My heart is like a singing bird
    Whose nest is in a watered shoot;
My heart is like an apple tree
    Whose boughs are bent with thickset fruit;
My heart is like a rainbow shell
    That paddles in a halcyon sea;
My heart is gladder than all these
    Because my love is come to me.

Raise me a dais of silk and down;
    Hang it with vair and purple dyes;
Carve it in doves and pomegranates,
    And peacocks with a hundred eyes;
Work it in gold and silver grapes,
    In leaves and silver fleurs-de-lys;
Because the birthday of my life
    Is come, my love is come to me.

Winter: My Secret

I tell my secret? No indeed, not I?
Perhaps some day, who knows?
But not today; it froze, and blows, and snows,
And you're too curious: fie!
You want to hear it? well:
Only, my secret's mine, and I won't tell.

Or, after all, perhaps there's none:
Suppose there is no secret after all,
But only just my fun.
Today's a nipping day, a biting day;
In which one wants a shawl,
A veil, a cloak, and other wraps:
I cannot ope to every one who taps,
And let the draughts come whistling thro' my hall;
Come bounding and surrounding me,
Come buffeting, astounding me,
Nipping and clipping thro' my wraps and all.
I wear my mask for warmth: who ever shows
His nose to Russian snows
To be pecked at by every wind that blows?
You would not peck? I thank you for good will,
Believe, but leave that truth untested still.

Spring's an expansive time: yet I don't trust
March with its peck of dust,
Nor April with its rainbow-crowned brief showers,
Nor even May, whose flowers
One frost may wither thro' the sunless hours.

Perhaps some languid summer day,
When drowsy birds sing less and less,
And golden fruit is ripening to excess,
If there's not too much sun nor too much cloud,
And the warm wind is neither still nor loud,

Perhaps my secret I may say,
    Or you may guess.

Maude Clare

Out of the church she followed them
    With a lofty step and mein:
His bride was like a village maid,
    Maude Clare was like a queen.

'Son Thomas,' his lady mother said,
    With smiles, almost with tears:
'May Nell and you but live as true
    As we have done for years;

'Your father thirty years ago
    Had just your tale to tell;
But he was not so pale as you,
    Nor I so pale as Nell.'

My lord was pale with inward strife,
    And Nell was pale with pride;
My lord gazed long on pale Maude Clare
    Or ever he kissed the bride.

'Lo, I have brought my gift, my lord,
    Have brought my gift,' she said:

'To bless the hearth, to bless the board,
    To bless the marriage-bed.

'Here's my half of the golden chain
    You wore about your neck,
That day we waded ankle-deep
    For lilies in the beck:

'Here's my half of the faded leaves
    We plucked from budding bough,
With feet amongst the lily leaves,—
    The lilies are budding now.'

He strove to match her scorn with scorn,
    He faltered in his place:
'Lady,' he said, – 'Maude Clare,' he said,—
    'Maude Clare:' – and hid his face.

She turn'd to Nell: 'My Lady Nell,
    I have a gift for you;
Tho' were it fruit, the bloom were gone,
    Or, were it flowers, the dew.

'Take my share of a fickle heart,
    Mine of a paltry love:
Take it or leave it as you will,
    I wash my hands thereof.'

'And what you leave,' said Nell, 'I'll take,
    And what you spurn, I'll wear;
For he's my lord for better and worse,
    And him I love, Maude Clare.

'Yea, tho' you're taller by the head,
    More wise, and much more fair;
I'll love him till he loves me best,
    Me best of all, Maude Clare.'

Up-hill

Does the road wind up-hill all the way?
    Yes, to the very end.

Will the day's journey take the whole long day?
    From morn to night, my friend.

But is there for the night a resting-place?
    A roof for when the slow dark hours begin.
May not the darkness hide it from my face?
    You cannot miss that inn.

Shall I meet other wayfarers at night?
    Those who have gone before.
Then must I knock, or call when just in sight?
    They will not keep you standing at that door.   9

Shall I find comfort, travel-sore and weak?
    Of labour you shall find the sum.
Will there be beds for me and all who seek?
    Yea, beds for all who come.

The Lowest Room

Like flowers sequestered from the sun
    And wind of summer, day by day
I dwindled paler, whilst my hair
    Showed the first tinge of grey.

'Oh what is life, that we should live?
    Or what is death, that we must die?
A bursting bubble is our life:
    I also, what am I?'

'What is your grief? now tell me, sweet,
    That I may grieve,' my sister said;
And stayed a white embroidering hand
    And raised a golden head:

Her tresses showed a richer mass,
    Her eyes looked softer than my own,
Her figure had a statelier height,
    Her voice a tenderer tone.

'Some must be second and not first;
    All cannot be the first of all:
Is not this, too, but vanity?
    I stumble like to fall.

'So yesterday I read the acts
    Of Hector and each clangorous king
With wrathful great Æacides:—
    Old Homer leaves a sting.'

The comely face looked up again,
    The deft hand lingered on the thread:
'Sweet, tell me what is Homer's sting,
    Old Homer's sting?' she said.

'He stirs my sluggish pulse like wine,
    He melts me like the wind of spice,
Strong as strong Ajax' red right hand,
    And grand like Juno's eyes.

'I cannot melt the sons of men,
    I cannot fire and tempest-toss:—
Besides, those days were golden days,
    Whilst these are days of dross.'

She laughed a feminine low laugh,
    Yet did not stay her dexterous hand:

'Now tell me of those days,' she said,
    'When time ran golden sand.'

'Then men were men of might and right,
    Sheer might, at least, and weighty swords;
Then men in open blood and fire
    Bore witness to their words,

'Crest-rearing kings with whistling spears; ·
    But if these shivered up in the shock
They wrenched up hundred-rooted trees,
    Or hurled the effacing rock.

'Then hand to hand, then foot to foot,
    Stern to the death-grip grappling then,
Who ever thought of gunpowder
    Amongst these men of men?

'They knew whose hand struck home the death,
    They knew who broke but would not bend,
Could venerate an equal foe
    And scorn a laggard friend.

'Calm in the utmost stress of doom,
    Devout toward adverse powers above,
They hated with intenser hate
    And loved with fuller love.

'Then heavenly beauty could allay
    As heavenly beauty stirred the strife:
By them a slave was worshipped more
        Than is by us a wife.'

She laughed again, my sister laughed;
    Made answer o'er the laboured cloth:
'I rather would be one of us
        Than wife, or slave, or both.'

'Oh better then be slave or wife
    Than fritter now blank life away:
Then night had holiness of night,
        And day was sacred day.

'The princess laboured at her loom,
    Mistress and handmaiden alike;
Beneath their needles grew the field
        With warriors armed to strike.

'Or, look again, dim Dian's face
    Gleamed perfect thro' the attendant night;
Were such not better than those holes
        Amid that waste of white?

'A shame it is, our aimless life:
    I rather from my heart would feed

From silver dish in gilded stall
    With wheat and wine the steed—

'The faithful steed that bore my lord
    In safety thro' the hostile land,
The faithful steed that arched his neck
    To fondle with my hand.'

Her needle erred; a moment's pause,
    A moment's patience, all was well.
Then she: 'But just suppose the horse,
    Suppose the rider fell?

'Then captive in an alien house,
    Hungering on exile's bitter bread,—
They happy, they who won the lot
    Of sacrifice,' she said.

Speaking she faltered, while her look
    Showed forth her passion like a glass:
With hand suspended, kindling eye,
    Flushed cheek, how fair she was!

'Ah well, be those the days of dross;
    This, if you will, the age of gold:
Yet had those days a spark of warmth,
    While these are somewhat cold—

'Are somewhat mean and cold and slow,
    Are stunted from heroic growth:
We gain but little when we prove
    The worthlessness of both.'

'But life is in our hands,' she said:
    'In our own hands for gain or loss:
Shall not the Sevenfold Sacred Fire
    Suffice to purge our dross?

'Too short a century of dreams,
    One day of work sufficient length:
Why should not you, why should not I
    Attain heroic strength?

'Our life is given us as a blank;
    Ourselves must make it blest or curst:
Who dooms me I shall only be
    The second, not the first?

'Learn from old Homer, if you will,
    Such wisdom as his books have said:
In one of the acts of Ajax shine,
    In one of Diomed.

'Honoured all heroes whose high deeds
    Thro' life, thro' death, enlarge their span:
Only Achilles in his rage
    And sloth is less than man.'

'Achilles only less than man?
    He less than man who, half a god,
Discomfited all Greece with rest,
    Cowed Ilion with a nod?

'He offered vengeance, lifelong grief
    To one dear ghost, uncounted price:
Beasts, Trojans, adverse gods, himself,
    Heaped up the sacrifice.

'Self-immolated to his friend,
    Shrined in world's wonder, Homer's page,
Is this the man, the less than men
    Of this degenerate age?'

'Gross from his acorns, tusky boar
    Does memorable acts like his;
So for her snared offended young
    Bleeds the swart lioness.'

But here she paused; our eyes had met,
    And I was whitening with the jeer;
She rose: 'I went too far,' she said;
    Spoke low: 'Forgive me, dear.

'To me our days seem pleasant days,
    Our home a haven of pure content;

Forgive me if I said too much,
  So much more than I meant.

'Homer, tho' greater than his gods,
  With rough-hewn virtues was sufficed
And rough-hewn men: but what are such
  To us who learn of Christ?'

The much-loved pathos of her voice,
  Her almost tearful eyes, her cheek
Grown pale, confessed the strength of love
  Which only made her speak:

For mild she was, of few soft words,
  Most gentle, easy to be led,
Content to listen when I spoke
  And reverence what I said;

I elder sister by six years;
  Not half so glad, or wise, or good:
Her words rebuked my secret self
  And shamed me where I stood.

She never guessed her words reproved
  A silent envy nursed within,
A selfish, souring discontent
  Pride-born, the devil's sin.

I smiled, half bitter, half in jest:
  'The wisest man of all the wise
Left for his summary of life
    "Vanity of vanities."

'Beneath the sun there's nothing new:
  Men flow, men ebb, mankind flows on:
If I am wearied of my life,
    Why so was Solomon.

'Vanity of vanities he preached
  Of all he found, of all he sought:
Vanity of vanities, the gist
    Of all the words he taught.

'This in the wisdom of the world,
  In Homer's page, in all, we find:
As the sea is not filled, so yearns
    Man's universal mind.

'This Homer felt, who gave his men
  With glory but a transient state:
His very Jove could not reverse
    Irrevocable fate.

'Uncertain all their lot save this—
  Who wins must lose, who lives must die:
All trodden out into the dark
    Alike, all vanity.'

She scarcely answered when I paused,
    But rather to herself said: 'One
Is here,' low-voiced and loving, 'Yea,
      Greater than Solomon.'

So both were silent, she and I:
    She laid her work aside, and went
Into the garden-walks, like spring.
      All gracious with content;

A little graver than her wont,
    Because her words had fretted me;
Not warbling quite her merriest tune
      Bird-like from tree to tree.

I chose a book to read and dream:
    Yet half the while with furtive eyes
Marked how she made her choice of flowers
      Intuitively wise,

And ranged them with instinctive taste
    Which all my books had failed to teach;
Fresh rose herself, and daintier
      Than blossom of the peach.

By birthright higher than myself,
    Tho' nestling of the selfsame nest:

No fault of hers, no fault of mine,
    But stubborn to digest.

I watched her, till my book unmarked
    Slid noiseless to the velvet floor;
Till all the opulent summer-world
    Looked poorer than before.

Just then her busy fingers ceased,
    Her fluttered colour went and came;
I knew whose step was on the walk,
    Whose voice would name her name.

          *   *   *

Well, twenty years have passed since then:
    My sister now, a stately wife
Still fair, looks back in peace and sees
    The longer half of life—

The longer half of prosperous life,
    With little grief, or fear, or fret:
She, loved and loving long ago,
    Is loved and loving yet.

A husband honourable, brave,
    Is her main wealth in all the world:

And next to him one like herself,
    One daughter golden-curled;

Fair image of her own fair youth,
    As beautiful and as serene,
With almost such another love
    As her own love has been.

Yet, tho' of world-wide charity,
    And in her home most tender dove,
Her treasure and her heart are stored
    In the home-land of love:

She thrives, God's blessed husbandry;
Most like a vine which full of fruit
Doth cling and lean and climb toward heaven
    While earth still binds its root.

I sit and watch my sister's face:
    How little altered since the hours
When she, a kind, light-hearted girl,
    Gathered her garden flowers;

Her song just mellowed by regret
    For having teased me with her talk;
Then all-forgetful as she heard
    One step upon the walk.

While I? I sat alone and watched;
    My lot in life, to live alone
In mine own world of interests,
    Much felt but little shown.

Not to be first: how hard to learn
    That lifelong lesson of the past;
Line graven on line and stroke on stroke;
    But, thank God, learned at last.

So now in patience I possess
    My soul year after tedious year,
Content to take the lowest place,
    The place assigned me here.

Yet sometimes, when I feel my strength
    Most weak, and life most burdensome,
I lift mine eyes up to the hills
    From whence my help shall come:

Yea, sometimes still I lift my heart
    To the Archangelic trumpet-burst,
When all deep secrets shall be shown,
    And many last be first.

Goblin Market

Morning and evening
Maids heard the goblins cry:
'Come buy our orchard fruits,
Come buy, come buy:
Apples and quinces,
Lemons and oranges,
Plump unpecked cherries,
Melons and raspberries,
Bloom-down-cheeked peaches,
Swart-headed mulberries,
Wild free-born cranberries,
Crab-apples, dewberries,
Pine-apples, blackberries,
Apricots, strawberries;—
All ripe together
In summer weather,—
Morns that pass by,
Fair eves that fly;
Come buy, come buy;
Our grapes fresh from the vine,
Pomegranates full and fine,
Dates and sharp bullaces,
Rare pears and greengages,
Damsons and bilberries,
Taste them and try:
Currants and gooseberries,

Bright-fire-like barberries,
Figs to fill your mouth,
Citrons from the South,
Sweet to tongue and sound to eye;
Come buy, come buy.'

Evening by evening
Among the brookside rushes,
Laura bowed her head to hear,
Lizzie veiled her blushes:
Crouching close together
In the cooling weather,
With clasping arms and cautioning lips,
With tingling cheeks and finger tips.
'Lie close,' Laura said,
Pricking up her golden head:
'We must not look at goblin men,
We must not buy their fruits:
Who knows upon what soil they fed
Their hungry thirsty roots?'
'Come buy,' call the goblins
Hobbling down the glen.
'Oh,' cried Lizzie, 'Laura, Laura,
You should not peep at goblin men.'
Lizzie covered up her eyes,
Covered close lest they should look;
Laura reared her glossy head,
And whispered like the restless brook:

'Look, Lizzie, look, Lizzie,
Down the glen tramp little men.
One hauls a basket,
One bears a plate,
One lugs a golden dish
Of many pounds weight.
How fair the vine must grow
Whose grapes are so luscious;
How warm the wind must blow
Thro' those fruit bushes.'
'No,' said Lizzie: 'No, no, no;
Their offers should not charm us,
Their evil gifts would harm us.'
She thrust a dimpled finger
In each ear, shut eyes and ran:
Curious Laura chose to linger
Wondering at each merchant man.
One had a cat's face,
One whisked a tail,
One tramped at a rat's pace,
One crawled like a snail,
One like a wombat prowled obtuse and furry,
One like a ratel tumbled hurry skurry.
She heard a voice like voice of doves
Cooing all together:
They sounded kind and full of loves
In the pleasant weather.

Laura stretched her gleaming neck
Like a rush-imbedded swan,
Like a lily from the beck,
Like a moonlit poplar branch,
Like a vessel at the launch
When its last restraint is gone.

Backwards up the mossy glen
Turned and trooped the goblin men,
With their shrill repeated cry,
'Come buy, come buy.'
When they reached where Laura was
They stood stock still upon the moss,
Leering at each other,
Brother and queer brother;
Signalling each other,
Brother with sly brother.
One set his basket down,
One reared his plate;
One began to weave a crown
Of tendrils, leaves and rough nuts brown
(Men sell not such in any town);
One heaved the golden weight
Of dish and fruit to offer her:
'Come buy, come buy,' was still their cry.
Laura stared but did not stir,
Longed but had no money:
The whisk-tailed merchant bade her taste

In tones as smooth as honey,
The cat-faced purr'd,
The rat-paced spoke a word
Of welcome, and the snail-paced even was heard;
One parrot-voiced and jolly
Cried 'Pretty Goblin' still for 'Pretty Polly;'—
One whistled like a bird.

But sweet-tooth Laura spoke in haste:
'Good folk, I have no coin;
To take were to purloin:
I have no copper in my purse,
I have no silver either,
And all my gold is on the furze
That shakes in windy weather
Above the rusty heather.'
'You have much gold upon your head,'
they answered all together:
'Buy from us with a golden curl.'
She clipped a precious golden lock,
She dropped a tear more rare than pearl,
Then sucked their fruit globes fair or red:
Sweeter than honey from the rock.
Stronger than man-rejoicing wine,
Clearer than water flowed that juice;
She never tasted such before,
How should it cloy with length of use?
She sucked and sucked and sucked the more

Fruits which that unknown orchard bore;
She sucked until her lips were sore;
Then flung the emptied rinds away
But gathered up one kernel-stone,
And knew not was it night or day
As she turned home alone.

Lizzie met her at the gate
Full of wise upbraidings:
'Dear, you should not stay so late,
Twilight is not good for maidens;
Should not loiter in the glen
In the haunts of goblin men.
Do you not remember Jeanie,
How she met them in the moonlight,
Took their gifts both choice and many,
Ate their fruits and wore their flowers
Plucked from bowers
Where summer ripens at all hours?
But ever in the noonlight
She pined and pined away;
Sought them by night and day,
Found them no more but dwindled and grew grey;
Then fell with the first snow,
While to this day no grass will grow
Where she lies now:
I planted daisies there a year ago
That never blow.

You should not loiter so.'
'Nay, hush,' said Laura:
'Nay, hush, my sister:
I ate and ate my fill,
Yet my mouth waters still;
Tomorrow night I will
Buy more:' and kissed her:
'Have done with sorrow;
I'll bring you plums tomorrow
Fresh on their mother twigs,
Cherries worth getting;
You cannot think what figs
My teeth have met in,
What melons icy-cold
Piled on a dish of gold
Too huge for me to hold,
What peaches with a velvet nap,
Pellucid grapes without one seed:
Odorous indeed must be the mead
Whereon they grow, and pure the wave they drink
With lilies at the brink,
And sugar-sweet their sap.'

Golden head by golden head,
Like two pigeons in one nest
Folded in each other's wings,
They lay down in their curtained bed:
Like two blossoms on one stem,

Like two flakes of new-fall'n snow,
Like two wands of ivory
Tipped with gold for awful kings.
Moon and stars gazed in at them,
Wind sang to them lullaby,
Lumbering owls forbore to fly,
Not a bat flapped to and fro
Round their rest:
Cheek to cheek and breast to breast
Locked together in one nest.

Early in the morning
When the first cock crowed his warning,
Neat like bees, as sweet and busy,
Laura rose with Lizzie:
Fetched in honey, milked the cows,
Aired and set to rights the house,
Kneaded cakes of whitest wheat,
Cakes for dainty mouths to eat,
Next churned butter, whipped up cream,
Fed their poultry, sat and sewed;
Talked as modest maidens should:
Lizzie with an open heart,
Laura in an absent dream,
One content, one sick in part;
One warbling for the mere bright day's delight,
One longing for the night.

At length slow evening came:
They went with pitchers to the reedy brook;
Lizzie most placid in her look,
Laura most like a leaping flame.
They drew the gurgling water from its deep;
Lizzie plucked purple and rich golden flags,
Then turning homewards said: 'The sunset flushes
Those furthest loftiest crags;
Come, Laura, not another maiden lags,
No wilful squirrel wags,
The beasts and birds are fast asleep.'
But Laura loitered still among the rushes
And said the bank was steep.

And said the hour was early still,
The dew not fall'n, the wind not chill:
Listening ever, but not catching
The customary cry,
'Come buy, come buy,'
With its iterated jingle
Of sugar-baited words:
Not for all her watching
Once discerning even one goblin
Racing, whisking, tumbling, hobbling;
Let alone the herds
That used to tramp along the glen,
In groups or single,
Of brisk fruit-merchant men.

Till Lizzie urged, 'O Laura, come;
I hear the fruit-call but I dare not look:
You should not loiter longer at this brook:
Come with me home.
The stars rise, the moon bends her arc,
Each glowworm winks her spark,
Let us get home before the night grows dark:
For clouds may gather
Tho' this is summer weather,
Put out the lights and drench us thro';
Then if we lost our way what should we do?'

Laura turned cold as stone
To find her sister heard that cry alone,
That goblin cry,
'Come buy our fruits, come buy.'
Must she then buy no more such dainty fruit?
Must she no more such succous pasture find,
Gone deaf and blind?
Her tree of life drooped from the root:
She said not one word in her heart's sore ache;
But peering thro' the dimness, nought discerning,
Trudged home, her pitcher dripping all the way;
So crept to bed, and lay
Silent till Lizzie slept;
Then sat up in a passionate yearning,
And gnashed her teeth for baulked desire, and wept
As if her heart would break.

Day after day, night after night,
Laura kept watch in vain
In sullen silence of exceeding pain.
She never caught again the goblin cry:
'Come buy, come buy;'—
She never spied the goblin men
Hawking their fruits along the glen:
But when the noon waxed bright
Her hair grew thin and grey;
She dwindled, as the fair full moon doth turn
To swift decay and burn
Her fire away.

One day remembering her kernel-stone
She set it by a wall that faced the south;
Dewed it with tears, hoped for a root,
Watched for a waxing shoot,
But there came none;
It never saw the sun,
It never felt the trickling moisture run:
While with sunk eyes and faded mouth
She dreamed of melons, as a traveller sees
False waves in desert drouth
With shade of leaf-crowned trees,
And burns the thirstier in the sandful breeze.

She no more swept the house,
Tended the fowls or cows,

Fetched honey, kneaded cakes of wheat,
Brought water from the brook:
But sat down listless in the chimney-nook
And would not eat.

Tender Lizzie could not bear
To watch her sister's cankerous care
Yet not to share.
She night and morning
Caught the goblins' cry:
'Come buy our orchard fruits,
Come buy, come buy:'—
Beside the brook, along the glen,
She heard the tramp of goblin men,
The voice and stir
Poor Laura could not hear;
Longed to buy fruit to comfort her,
But feared to pay too dear.
She thought of Jeanie in her grave,
Who should have been a bride;
But who for joys brides hope to have
Fell sick and died
In her gay prime,
In earliest Winter time,
With the first glazing rime,
With the first snow-fall of crisp Winter time.

Till Laura dwindling
Seemed knocking at Death's door:
Then Lizzie weighed no more
Better and worse;
But put a silver penny in her purse,
Kissed Laura, crossed the heath with clumps of furze
At twilight, halted by the brook:
And for the first time in her life
Began to listen and look.

Laughed every goblin
When they spied her peeping:
Came towards her hobbling,
Flying, running, leaping,
Puffing and blowing,
Chuckling, clapping, crowing,
Clucking and gobbling,
Mopping and mowing,
Full of airs and graces,
Pulling wry faces,
Demure grimaces,
Cat-like and rat-like,
Ratel- and wombat-like,
Snail-paced in a hurry,
Parrot-voiced and whistler,
Helter skelter, hurry skurry,
Chattering like magpies,
Fluttering like pigeons,

Gliding like fishes,—
Hugged her and kissed her,
Squeezed and caressed her:
Stretched up their dishes,
Panniers, and plates:
'Look at our apples
Russet and dun,
Bob at our cherries,
Bite at our peaches,
Citrons and dates,
Grapes for the asking,
Pears red with basking
Out in the sun,
Plums on their twigs;
Pluck them and suck them,
Pomegranates, figs.'—

'Good folk,' said Lizzie,
Mindful of Jeanie:
'Give me much and many:'—
Held out her apron,
Tossed them her penny.
'Nay, take a seat with us,
Honour and eat with us,'
They answered grinning:
'Our feast is but beginning.
Night yet is early,
Warm and dew-pearly,

Wakeful and starry:
Such fruits as these
No man can carry;
Half their bloom would fly,
Half their dew would dry,
Half their flavour would pass by.
Sit down and feast with us,
Be welcome guest with us,
Cheer you and rest with us.'—
'Thank you,' said Lizzie: 'But one waits
At home alone for me:
So without further parleying,
If you will not sell me any
Of your fruits tho' much and many,
Give me back my silver penny
I tossed you for a fee.'—
They began to scratch their pates,
No longer wagging, purring,
But visibly demurring,
Grunting and snarling.
One called her proud,
Cross-grained, uncivil;
Their tones waxed loud,
Their looks were evil.
Lashing their tails
They trod and hustled her,
Elbowed and jostled her,
Clawed with their nails,

Barking, mewing, hissing, mocking,
Tore her gown and soiled her stocking,
Twitched her hair out by the roots,
Stamped upon her tender feet,
Held her hands and squeezed their fruits
Against her mouth to make her eat.
White and golden Lizzie stood,
Like a lily in a flood,—
Like a rock of blue-veined stone
Lashed by tides obstreperously,—
Like a beacon left alone
In a hoary roaring sea,
Sending up a golden fire,—
Like a fruit-crowned orange-tree
White with blossoms honey-sweet
Sore beset by wasp and bee,—
Like a royal virgin town
Topped with gilded dome and spire
Close beleaguered by a fleet
Mad to tug her standard down.

One may lead a horse to water,
Twenty cannot make him drink.
Tho' the goblins cuffed and caught her,
Coaxed and fought her,
Bullied and besought her,
Scratched her, pinched her black as ink,
Kicked and knocked her,

Mauled and mocked her,
Lizzie uttered not a word;
Would not open lip from lip
Lest they should cram a mouthful in:
But laughed in heart to feel the drip
Of juice that syrupped all her face,
And lodged in dimples of her chin,
And streaked her neck which quaked like curd.
At last the evil people
Worn out by her resistance
Flung back her penny, kicked their fruit
Along whichever road they took,
Not leaving root or stone or shoot;
Some writhed into the ground,
Some dived into the brook
With ring and ripple,
Some scudded on the gale without a sound,
Some vanished in the distance.
In a smart, ache, tingle,
Lizzie went her way;
Knew not was it night or day;
Sprang up the bank, tore thro' the furze,
Threaded copse and dingle,
And heard her penny jingle
Bouncing in her purse,
Its bounce was music to her ear.
She ran and ran
As if she feared some goblin man

Dogged her with gibe or curse
Or something worse:
But not one goblin skurried after,
Nor was she pricked by fear;
The kind heart made her windy-paced
That urged her home quite out of breath with haste
And inward laughter.

She cried 'Laura,' up the garden,
'Did you miss me?
Come and kiss me.
Never mind my bruises,
Hug me, kiss me, suck my juices
Squeezed from goblin fruits for you,
Goblin pulp and goblin dew.
Eat me, drink me, love me;
Laura, make much of me:
For your sake I have braved the glen
And had to do with goblin merchant men.'

Laura started from her chair,
Flung her arms up in the air,
Clutched her hair:
'Lizzie, Lizzie, have you tasted
For my sake the fruit forbidden?
Must your light like mine be hidden,
Your young life like mine be wasted,
Undone in mine undoing

And ruined in my ruin,
Thirsty, cankered, goblin-ridden?'—
She clung about her sister,
Kissed and kissed and kissed her:
Tears once again
Refreshed her shrunken eyes,
Dropping like rain
After long sultry drouth;
Shaking with aguish fear, and pain,
She kissed and kissed her with a hungry mouth.

Her lips began to scorch,
That juice was wormwood to her tongue,
She loathed the feast:
Writhing as one possessed she leaped and sung,
Rent all her robe, and wrung
Her hands in lamentable haste,
And beat her breast.
Her locks streamed like the torch
Borne by a racer at full speed,
Or like the mane of horses in their flight,
Or like an eagle when she stems the light
Straight toward the sun,
Or like a caged thing freed,
Or like a flying flag when armies run.

Swift fire spread thro' her veins, knocked at her heart,
Met the fire smouldering there

And overbore its lesser flame;
She gorged on bitterness without a name:
Ah! fool, to choose such part
Of soul-consuming care!
Sense failed in the mortal strife:
Like the watch-tower of a town
Which an earthquake shatters down,
Like a lightning-stricken mast,
Like a wind-uprooted tree
Spun about,
Like a foam-topped waterspout
Cast down headlong in the sea,
She fell at last;
Pleasure past and anguish past,
Is it death or is it life?

Life out of death.
That night long Lizzie watched by her,
Counted her pulse's flagging stir,
Felt for her breath,
Held water to her lips, and cooled her face
With tears and fanning leaves:
But when the first birds chirped about their eaves,
And early reapers plodded to the place
Of golden sheaves,
And dew-wet grass
Bowed in the morning winds so brisk to pass,
And new buds with new day

Opened of cup-like lilies on the stream,
Laura awoke as from a dream,
Laughed in the innocent old way,
Hugged Lizzie but not twice or thrice;
Her gleaming locks showed not one thread of grey,
Her breath was sweet as May
And light danced in her eyes.

Days, weeks, months, years
Afterwards, when both were wives
With children of their own;
Their mother-hearts beset with fears,
Their lives bound up in tender lives;
Laura would call the little ones
And tell them of her early prime,
Those pleasant days long gone
Of not-returning time:
Would talk about the haunted glen,
The wicked, quaint fruit-merchant men,
Their fruits like honey to the throat
But poison in the blood;
(Men sell not such in any town:)
Would tell them how her sister stood,
In deadly peril to do her good,
And win the fiery antidote:
Then joining hands to little hands
Would bid them cling together,
'For there is no friend like a sister

In calm or stormy weather;
To cheer one on the tedious way,
To fetch one if one goes astray,
To lift one if one totters down,
To strengthen whilst one stands.'

'Who has seen the wind?'

Who has seen the wind?
　　Neither I nor you:
But when the leaves hang trembling
　　The wind is passing thro'.

Who has seen the wind?
　　Neither you nor I:
But when the trees bow down their heads
　　The wind is passing by.

A Christmas Carol

In the bleak mid-winter
   Frosty wind made moan,
Earth stood hard as iron,
   Water like a stone;
Snow has fallen, snow on snow,
   Snow on snow,
In the bleak mid-winter
   Long ago.

Our God, Heaven cannot hold Him
   Nor earth sustain;
Heaven and earth shall flee away
   When He comes to reign:
In the bleak mid-winter
   A stable-place sufficed
The Lord God Almighty
   Jesus Christ.

Enough for Him whom cherubim
   Worship night and day,
A breastful of milk
   And a mangerful of hay;
Enough for Him whom angels
   Fall down before,
The ox and ass and camel
   Which adore.

Angels and archangels
    May have gathered there,
Cherubim and seraphim
    Throng'd the air,
But only His mother
    In her maiden bliss
Worshipped the Beloved
    With a kiss.

What can I give Him,
    Poor as I am?
If I were a shepherd
    I would bring a lamb,
If I were a wise man
    I would do my part,—
Yet what I can I give Him,
    Give my heart.

Monna innominata

A SONNET OF SONNETS

I

'*Lo dì che han detto a' dolci amici addio.*'

DANTE

'*Amor, con quanto sforzo oggi mi vinci!*'

PETRARCA

Come back to me, who wait and watch for you:—
   Or come not yet, for it is over then,
   And long it is before you come again,
So far between my pleasures are and few.
While, when you come not, what I do I do
   Thinking 'Now when he comes,' my sweetest 'when:'
   For one man is my world of all the men
This wide world holds; O love, my world is you.
Howbeit, to meet you grows almost a pang
   Because the pang of parting comes so soon;
My hope hangs waning, waxing, like a moon
   Between the heavenly days on which we meet:
Ah me, but where are now the songs I sang
   When life was sweet because you called them sweet?

2

'Era già l'ora che volge il desio.'

DANTE

'Ricorro al tempo ch'io vi vidi prima.'

PETRARCA

I wish I could remember that first day,
  First hour, first moment of your meeting me,
  If bright or dim the season, it might be
Summer or Winter for aught I can say;
So unrecorded did it slip away,
  So blind was I to see and to foresee,
  So dull to mark the budding of my tree
That would not blossom yet for many a May.
If only I could recollect it, such
  A day of days! I let it come and go
  As traceless as a thaw of bygone snow;
It seemed to mean so little, meant so much;
If only now I could recall that touch,
  First touch of hand in hand – Did one but know!

3

'O ombre vane, fuor che ne l'aspetto!'

DANTE

'Immaginata guida la conduce.'

PETRARCA

I dream of you to wake: would that I might
   Dream of you and not wake but slumber on;
    Nor find with dreams the dear companion gone,
As Summer ended Summer birds take flight.
In happy dreams I hold you full in sight,
   I blush again who waking look so wan;
    Brighter than sunniest day that ever shone,
In happy dreams your smile makes day of night.
Thus only in a dream we are at one,
   Thus only in a dream we give and take
    The faith that maketh rich who take or give;
If thus to sleep is sweeter than to wake,
    To die were surely sweeter than to live,
Tho' there be nothing new beneath the sun.

4

'Poca favilla gran fiamma seconda.'

DANTE

'Ogni altra cosa, ogni pensier va fore,
E sol ivi con voi rimansi amore.'

PETRARCA

I loved you first: but afterwards your love
   Outsoaring mine, sang such a loftier song
As drowned the friendly cooings of my dove.
   Which owes the other most? my love was long,
   And yours one moment seemed to wax more strong;
I loved and guessed at you, you construed me
And loved me for what might or might not be—
   Nay, weights and measures do us both a wrong.
For verily love knows not 'mine' or 'thine;'
   With separate 'I' and 'thou' free love has done,
   For one is both and both are one in love:
Rich love knows nought of 'thine that is not mine;'
   Both have the strength and both the length thereof,
   Both of us, of the love which makes us one.

'*Amor che a nulla amato amar perdona.*'

DANTE

'*Amor m'addusse in sì gioiosa spene.*'

PETRARCA

O my heart's heart, and you who are to me
   More than myself myself, God be with you,
   Keep you in strong obedience leal and true
To Him whose noble service setteth free,
Give you all good we see or can foresee,
   Make your joys many and your sorrows few,
   Bless you in what you hear and what you do,
Yea, perfect you as He would have you be,
So much for you; but what for me, dear friend?
   To love you without stint and all I can
Today, tomorrow, world without an end;
     To love you much and yet to love you more,
   As Jordan at his flood sweeps either shore;
Since woman is the helpmeet made for man.

6

'Or puoi la quantitate
Comprender de l'amor che a te mi scalda.'

DANTE

'Non vo'che da tal nodo amor mi sciolglia.'

PETRARCA

Trust me, I have not earned your dear rebuke,
  I love, as you would have me, God the most;
    Would lose not Him, but you, must one be lost,
Nor with Lot's wife cast back a faithless look
Unready to forego what I forsook;
    This say I, having counted up the cost,
    This, tho' I be the feeblest of God's host,
The sorriest sheep Christ shepherds with His crook.
Yet while I love my God the most, I deem
    That I can never love you overmuch;
      I love Him more, so let me love you too;
    Yea, as I apprehend it, love is such
I cannot love you if I love not Him,
      I cannot love Him if I love not you.

'*Qui primavera sempre ed ogni frutto.*'

DANTE

'*Ragionando con meco ed io con lui.*'

PETRARCA

'Love me, for I love you' – and answer me,
  'Love me, for I love you' – so shall we stand
  As happy equals in the flowering land
Of love, that knows not a dividing sea.
Love builds the house on rock and not on sand,
  Love laughs what while the winds rave desperately;
And who hath found love's citadel unmanned?
  And who hath held in bonds love's liberty?
My heart's a coward tho' my words are brave—
  We meet so seldom, yet we surely part
  So often; there's a problem for your art!
    Still I find comfort in his Book, who saith,
Tho' jealousy be cruel as the grave,
    And death be strong, yet love is strong as death.

8

'*Come dicesse a Dio: D'altro non calme.*'

DANTE

'*Spero trovar pietà non che perdono.*'

PETRARCA

'I, if I perish, perish' – Esther spake:
    And bride of life or death she made her fair
    In all the lustre of her perfumed hair
And smiles that kindle longing but to slake.
She put on pomp of loveliness, to take
    Her husband thro' his eyes at unaware;
    She spread abroad her beauty for a snare,
Harmless as doves and subtle as a snake.
She trapped him with one mesh of silken hair,
    She vanquished him by wisdom of her wit,
        And built her people's house that it should stand:—
If I might take my life so in my hand,
And for my love to Love put up my prayer,
    And for love's sake by Love be granted it!

9

'O dignitosa coscienza e netta!'

DANTE

'Spirto più acceso di virtuti ardenti.'

PETRARCA

Thinking of you, and all that was, and all
   That might have been and now can never be,
   I feel your honoured excellence, and see
Myself unworthy of the happier call:
For woe is me who walk so apt to fall,
   So apt to shrink afraid, so apt to flee,
   Apt to lie down and die (ah, woe is me!)
Faithless and hopeless turning to the wall.
And yet not hopeless quite nor faithless quite,
Because not loveless; love may toil all night,
   But take at morning; wrestle till the break
      Of day, but then wield power with God and man: —
      So take I heart of grace as best I can,
   Ready to spend and be spent for your sake.

'*Con miglior corso e con migliore stella.*'

DANTE

'*La vita fugge e non s'arresta un' ora.*'

PETRARCA

Time flies, hope flags, life plies a wearied wing;
　　Death following hard on life gains ground apace;
　　Faith runs with each and rears an eager face,
Outruns the rest, makes light of everything,
Spurns earth, and still finds breath to pray and sing;
　　While love ahead of all uplifts his praise,
　　Still asks for grace and still gives thanks for grace,
Content with all day brings and night will bring.
Life wanes; and when love folds his wings above
　　Tired hope, and less we feel his conscious pulse,
　　　Let us go fall asleep, dear friend, in peace:
　　A little while, and age and sorrow cease;
　　A little while, and life reborn annuls
Loss and decay and death, and all is love.

11

'Vien dietro a me e lascia dir le genti.'

DANTE

'Contando i casi della vita nostra.'

PETRARCA

Many in aftertimes will say of you
   'He loved her' – while of me what will they say?
   Not that I loved you more than just in play,
For fashion's sake as idle women do.
Even let them prate; who know not what we knew
   Of love and parting in exceeding pain,
   Of parting hopeless here to meet again,
Hopeless on earth, and heaven is out of view.
But by my heart of love laid bare to you,
   My love that you can make not void nor vain,
Love that foregoes you but to claim anew
     Beyond this passage of the gate of death,
   I charge you at the Judgment make it plain
     My love of you was life and not a breath.

'*Amor, che ne la mente mi ragiona.*'

DANTE

'*Amor vien nel bel viso di costei.*'

PETRARCA

If there be any one can take my place
   And make you happy whom I grieve to grieve,
   Think not that I can grudge it, but believe
I do commend you to that nobler grace,
That readier wit than mine, that sweeter face;
   Yea, since your riches made me rich, conceive
   I too am crowned, while bridal crowns I weave,
And thread the bridal dance with jocund pace.
For if I did not love you, it might be
   That I should grudge you some one dear delight;
     But since the heart is yours that was mine own,
   Your pleasure is my pleasure, right my right,
Your honourable freedom makes me free,
     And you companioned I am not alone.

13

'E drizzeremo glí occhi al Primo Amore.'
DANTE

'Ma trovo peso non de la mie braccia.'
PETRARCA

If I could trust mine own self with your fate,
   Shall I not rather trust it in God's hand?
   Without Whose Will one lily doth not stand,
Nor sparrow fall at his appointed date;
   Who numbereth the innumerable sand,
Who weighs the wind and water with a weight,
To Whom the world is neither small nor great,
   Whose knowledge foreknew every plan we planned.
Searching my heart for all that touches you,
   I find there only love and love's goodwill
Helpless to help and impotent to do,
     Of understanding dull, of sight most dim;
     And therefore I commend you back to Him
Whose love your love's capacity can fill.

'*E la Sua Volontade è nostra pace.*'

DANTE

'*Sol con questi pensier, con altre chiome.*'

PETRARCA

Youth gone, and beauty gone if ever there
　　Dwelt beauty in so poor a face as this;
　　Youth gone and beauty, what remains of bliss?
I will not bind fresh roses in my hair,
To shame a cheek at best but little fair,—
　　Leave youth his roses, who can bear a thorn,—
I will not seek for blossoms anywhere,
　　Except such common flowers as blow with corn.
Youth gone and beauty gone, what doth remain?
　　The longing of a heart pent up forlorn,
　　　A silent heart whose silence loves and longs;
　　　The silence of a heart which sang its songs
　　While youth and beauty made a summer morn,
Silence of love that cannot sing again.